The Tao of the Spiritual Warrior

Cristy

ISBN: 979-8-218-08077-8

Printed by Spiritual Warrior Publishing

Edited by John Rickards, https://johnrickards.com/.

The Tao of the Spiritual Warrior

Overcome personal challenges and obstacles in order to achieve a higher level of spiritual awareness.

A spiritual warrior is someone who strives to live in harmony with the natural world and to cultivate inner peace and balance.

The emphasis is on the importance of living in accordance with the natural flow of the universe, known as the Tao. This means letting go of the ego and the desire for control, and instead allowing oneself to be guided by the natural rhythms of the world.

To achieve this state of spiritual harmony, one must cultivate certain virtues, such as humility, compassion, and inner peace. The spiritual warrior must also be willing to let go of attachments and ego-driven desires, and to embrace a life of simplicity and mindfulness.

In addition to these internal practices, the spiritual warrior emphasizes the importance of living in harmony with others and with the natural world. This means treating others with kindness and respect, and taking care of the environment and all living beings.

By following this path, the spiritual warrior seeks to achieve a state of enlightenment and inner fulfillment.

The Tao of the warrior is living by design, not by accident.—Dan Millman

As a spiritual warrior, you are someone who is purposeful and intentional in your actions, rather than simply reacting to circumstances or going through life by accident. You are guided by a clear set of principles and values, where you make conscious and deliberate choices in your life in order to live in alignment with them. By living by design rather than by accident, you are able to navigate the challenges and opportunities of life with greater clarity and purpose.

A spiritual warrior is dedicated to the pursuit of spiritual growth and development. This means you must work to overcome personal challenges and obstacles in order to achieve a higher level of spiritual awareness. You may also engage in spiritual practices such as meditation, prayer, and self-reflection.

As a spiritual warrior, you are often seen as someone who is strong and resilient, both mentally and emotionally, and who is willing to confront and overcome obstacles and challenges in order to grow and evolve spiritually. You are also seen as someone who is committed to living in accordance with their spiritual beliefs and values, and who is willing to defend and protect these beliefs and values against external threats or challenges.

Overall, as a spiritual warrior you are dedicated to personal growth and development, both on a spiritual level and in other areas of life. It is about striving to become the best version of yourself.

If these concepts do not currently describe or resonate with you, you need to better understand the principles you must adhere to put you on the path—or the way of the spiritual warrior.

In the Beginning

As children, our brains are still developing and we have limited cognitive abilities compared to adults. This can make us more susceptible to indoctrination, as we may not have the ability to think critically or evaluate information in the way that adults can. Because of this, it is important for adults to provide children with accurate and balanced information, and to encourage critical thinking and independent thinking from a young age. This can help to prevent children from being easily swayed by biased or misleading information as well as helping them to develop the skills they need to resist indoctrination as they grow older.

Indoctrination is the process of teaching someone to accept a set of beliefs or values or presenting ideas as absolute truths without any opportunity for questioning or critical thinking. In the context of children, indoctrination can occur when parents, teachers, or other influential figures in a child's life attempt to shape their beliefs and values in a certain way, often without providing them with the opportunity to question or challenge those beliefs. This can happen in a variety of ways, such as through the use of propaganda, religious teachings, or other forms of persuasive language and behavior. Shaping their beliefs and values in a certain direction can lead to the development of deeply-held convictions that may be difficult to change later in life.

Indoctrination can have both positive and negative effects, depending on the beliefs and values being taught. In some cases, it may help to instill important moral values or principles in children, such as honesty, compassion, and respect. However, it can also be used to propagate harmful or misguided beliefs, such as prejudice, intolerance, or extremist ideologies. It can also limit a person's ability to consider other viewpoints and to engage in open-minded and respectful dialogue with people who hold different beliefs.

Every Journey Starts with a Single Step

It is important for anyone, but in particular a young person, to think critically for themselves because it helps you develop your own beliefs and opinions and to analyze and evaluate information and ideas, rather than simply accepting them at face value.

To set yourself on the path of a spiritual warrior, start by encouraging yourself to think critically. It's an important part of helping you to become an independent and open-minded individual who is able to make your own decisions. It is a valuable skill that can benefit you throughout your life.

If the people who influence you, no matter what age you are, do not encourage you to think critically about your decisions, you must find the courage to think for yourself and challenge any negative thoughts or emotions that may be holding you back from finding the best path for you.

The Purpose of Life

The two most important days in your life are the day you are born and the day you find out why.— Mark Twain

The search for purpose or meaning in your life is an ongoing journey that may not always be clear or easy. It suggests that you must be open to new experiences and opportunities, and be willing to seek out what truly resonates with you in order to find your own unique path and purpose in life. Ultimately, the reason for our existence may be different for each person, and it is up to each of us to discover our own unique meaning and purpose in life.

It is difficult for us to fully comprehend the reason behind our existence. One theory is that our purpose is simply to reproduce and ensure the continuation of our species. Some people believe in a higher power as an explanation for things that are not well understood. Many individuals tend to follow the path that offers the most benefits with the least amount of effort, as it is a natural human tendency. Some people also assume that they will live forever or have an opportunity to live over again, which may lead them to live a less fulfilling life because they believe they will be rewarded in the afterlife.

However, these beliefs may not be accurate. We are born, influenced by the beliefs and values of those around us, and make choices based on these influences. Eventually, we all pass away. It is the choices we make during our lifetime that determine whether our lives are filled with suffering or are healthy and happy. By choosing the path of the spiritual warrior, we can live life intentionally and strive for the greatest rewards, even if it requires sustained effort and involves overcoming various challenges and obstacles.

The Ten Tenets

Indecision and poor decision-making can significantly impede our efforts to live a fulfilling and healthy life. To overcome this challenge, it can be helpful to establish a set of personal guiding principles that have developed over time and are specific to you. These principles should be mutually exclusive, which means they should not conflict with one another, to make decision-making easier. When faced with a decision, consider whether it aligns with one of your guiding principles. This can help you make choices that are consistent with your values and goals.

Our ancestors also had a system in place, that still currently persists, for guiding their actions and decision-making. They believed in a deity who provided a set of rules for all people to follow, one example being the Ten Commandments. These rules function like guiding principles, but they apply to everyone and are not specific to each individual. For example, one of your personal guiding principles might be to always strive to give back more than you take in any given situation, while another could be to seek out opportunities to learn and share knowledge with others. You could also include a sense of humor as one of your guiding principles, such as not taking life too seriously because we will all eventually pass away. In the mean-time let the path of the spiritual warrior provide you with not only happiness, but exuberance.

There are many different sets of principles or values that people may choose to live by, and what is considered important or essential can vary greatly depending on individual beliefs and circumstances. However, some common principles or values that many people may find helpful to live by include:

1. Honesty and integrity: being truthful and transparent in all your actions and interactions, and treating others with respect and fairness.
2. Compassion and empathy: showing understanding and concern for others, and being willing to help those in need.
3. Respect for others: valuing the dignity and worth of every person, and treating them with kindness and consideration.

4. Responsibility and accountability: taking ownership of your actions and decisions, and being willing to accept the consequences of your choices.
5. Perseverance and determination: staying focused and committed to your goals, and never giving up, even in the face of challenges or setbacks.
6. Gratitude and appreciation: being thankful for the good things in your life, and expressing gratitude to others for their help and support.
7. Humility and modesty: recognizing your own limitations and flaws, and being willing to learn from others and improve yourself.
8. Forgiveness and understanding: letting go of anger, resentment, and bitterness, and being willing to forgive others and yourself.
9. Courage and bravery: standing up for what is right and just, and being willing to take risks and face challenges in pursuit of your goals.
10. Love and kindness: showing love and affection to those around you, and being willing to extend kindness and generosity to others, even when it is difficult or inconvenient.

Again, these are just some examples of principles or values that people may choose to live by. Ultimately, the specific principles or values that are most important to you will depend on your own beliefs and priorities, and what you consider to be most meaningful and valuable in your life.

For example, if one of your guiding principles is to always be honest and transparent in your communication, it can help you make decisions about whether to tell the truth or not. Similarly, if one of your principles is to prioritize your physical and mental health, it can help you make decisions about whether to engage in activities that support your well-being or not.

Having a clear set of guiding principles can also help to reduce cognitive dissonance, which is the psychological discomfort that occurs when we hold conflicting beliefs or values. By aligning your actions with your guiding principles, you can avoid situations where your beliefs and actions are in conflict, which can lead to feelings of discomfort and confusion, or even illness.

Overall, having a small set of guiding principles can help you make decisions more easily and lead a healthy and productive life. It can also provide a sense of direction and purpose, and help you stay true to your values and goals.

Living Deliberately

Living deliberately refers to the idea of intentionally choosing how you live your life, rather than allowing external circumstances or other people to dictate your actions and decisions. It involves being conscious and aware of your choices, and taking responsibility for the direction of your life, rather than simply reacting to events or following the path of least resistance.

Living deliberately requires a certain level of self-awareness and self-reflection, as well as the willingness to take action and make difficult choices in pursuit of your goals and values. It also involves setting clear intentions and priorities, and making decisions that are aligned with those intentions, rather than simply going along with the status quo or following the expectations of others.

Living deliberately can have many positive benefits, including a greater sense of control and agency over your life, as well as increased fulfillment and satisfaction. It can also help to reduce stress and anxiety, by giving you a sense of direction and purpose, and by allowing you to focus on the things that are most important to you.

The mass of men lead lives of quiet desperation.—Henry David Thoreau

Many people go through life feeling trapped and unfulfilled, simply going through the motions and not living with purpose or intention. The quote from Thoreau encourages us to live deliberately, to make conscious choices about how we live our lives and to find meaning and purpose in our pursuits. By living deliberately, we can break free from the "quiet desperation" of a meaningless existence and find greater fulfillment and happiness in life.

Always have an Edge

Gaining an edge in life, at work, or in general refers to the idea of gaining an advantage over others in a particular situation or context. This can take many forms, and can involve a variety of different strategies and tactics. Some common ways of gaining an edge in various situations include:

- Developing new skills or knowledge, constantly striving to improve your abilities in your field or area of expertise. By staying up to date with the latest developments and trends, and by continually learning and growing, you can give yourself an advantage over others who are not as knowledgeable or skilled.

- Building strong relationships with others, both inside and outside of your organization. By establishing positive connections with key stakeholders and influencers, you can gain access to valuable resources, information, and opportunities that can help you to succeed.
- Being proactive and strategic in your approach to challenges and opportunities. This can involve anticipating potential obstacles or issues, and developing plans to overcome them, as well as identifying and pursuing opportunities that others may not have noticed or considered.
- Maintaining a positive attitude and mindset even in the face of challenges or setbacks. By staying focused and motivated, and by remaining resilient and optimistic, you can give yourself an advantage over others who may become discouraged or lose sight of their goals.

By taking action to improve your skills, knowledge, and relationships, and to be proactive and strategic in your approach to challenges and opportunities. You can give yourself an advantage over others, and increase your chances of success.

Seeking the Approval of Strangers

Seeking the approval of strangers can be a common and natural desire, especially in today's social media-driven world, where it can be tempting to seek validation from others in the form of likes, comments, or followers. However, this can also be a potential pitfall, as relying on the approval of strangers can be detrimental to your well-being and happiness in a number of ways.

For one thing, it can lead to a lack of authenticity and vulnerability. In order to gain approval from others, you may be tempted to present a carefully curated image of yourself, rather than being open and honest about who you really are. This can lead to a disconnect between your online persona and your true self, which can be emotionally and mentally exhausting to maintain.

It can also lead to a lack of self-esteem and self-worth. When your self-worth is based on the approval of others, you can become dependent on their validation to feel good about yourself. This can make you vulnerable to the whims and opinions of others, and can leave you feeling empty and unfulfilled if you do not receive the approval you crave.

Finally, it can be a time-consuming and distracting pursuit, which can take away from other more meaningful and fulfilling aspects of your life. When you are constantly seeking approval from others, it can be difficult to focus on your own goals and priorities, and to pursue activities and experiences that are personally enriching and fulfilling. Instead, you may find yourself constantly checking your social media feeds, obsessing over your appearance or public image, or comparing yourself to others, which can be emotionally and mentally draining.

> The approval of others is a dangerous addiction. It will never give you the feeling of satisfaction you are seeking. The only approval you need is your own."—Steve Maraboli

Seeking the approval of others is a futile pursuit, as it will never truly satisfy us. Instead, it is important to find approval and validation within yourself and to focus on your own values and goals. This can help you to build self-confidence and self-worth, and to live a more authentic and fulfilling life.

Losing Self-Importance

Losing self-importance refers to the idea of letting go of the belief that you are superior or more important than others. This can be a difficult and challenging process, as our egos often crave recognition, validation, and admiration from others. However, letting go of self-importance can also have many benefits, both for ourselves and for those around us.

It can help us to develop a more realistic and humble view of ourselves. When we are consumed by self-importance, we may tend to exaggerate our own abilities, accomplishments, or qualities, and to dismiss or downplay those of others. By letting go of self-importance, we can gain a more balanced and accurate perspective on ourselves and our place in the world.

It can also help us to develop greater empathy and compassion for others. When we are consumed by self-importance, we may tend to see others as inferior or lesser than ourselves, and to treat them with disdain or disrespect. By letting go of self-importance, we can open ourselves up to the experiences and perspectives of others, and to develop a greater understanding and compassion for their struggles and challenges.

Finally, it can help us to build stronger and more authentic relationships with others. When we are consumed by self-importance, we may tend to see others as objects to be used or manipulated for our own gain, rather than as individuals with their own needs, feelings, and desires. By letting go of self-importance, we can develop more genuine and respectful connections with others, which can be personally and socially enriching.

The spiritual warrior is not one who seeks power over others, but rather seeks to empower themselves and others through compassion, understanding, and kindness. They understand that true strength comes from within, and seek to use their inner power to create positive change in the world.

We either make ourselves miserable, or we make ourselves strong. The amount of work is the same—Carlos Castaneda

We have a choice in how we approach our lives and the challenges we face. If we focus on our own ego and self-importance, we may feel miserable and overwhelmed by life's challenges. However, if we let go of our ego and focus on becoming stronger and more resilient, we can overcome those challenges and find meaning and purpose in life.

The concept of removing ego and avoiding confrontation unless absolutely necessary is based on the idea that ego can be a hindrance in many situations. Ego is the sense of self-importance or self-esteem that individuals often possess, and it can cause them to behave in ways that are selfish or aggressive. In some cases, ego can lead individuals to engage in confrontations that could be avoided, simply because they feel the need to assert their own importance.

One way to avoid confrontations is to remove ego from the equation and to focus on finding peaceful solutions to conflicts. This might involve things like compromising, negotiating, or simply walking away from a confrontation if it appears that it cannot be resolved peacefully.

Of course, there are times when it may be necessary to fight or to engage in confrontation. In these cases, it is important to do so only as a last resort, and to approach the situation with a clear head and a calm demeanor. By remaining focused and composed, individuals can better defend themselves and others. By removing ego from the equation and focusing on peaceful solutions, you can avoid getting caught up in unnecessary conflicts and can instead focus on finding mutually beneficial solutions. Given this exchange,

> Callie blasts through the door and demands, "You can't park there, that's a visitor spot." Driven by ego, you might consider confronting her which could lead to escalation and an unpleasant experience for both of you. Instead, remove ego, and respond: "Callie, I understand that you need to enforce the rules about parking in visitor spots. I apologize for parking there earlier. I was unable to find an available spot and didn't mean to cause any issues. In the future, I will be more careful to make sure I park in a designated spot."

a potential conflict was resolved by showing humility.

Another way to avoid conflicts is to not engage with people who have negative intentions:

> As Elena sat working on her laptop in the team room, a coworker she barely knew sat down next to her and said "I don't like you." Elena simply replied "It doesn't matter to me" without even looking at her colleague. Her coworker stood up in anger and left.

Elena's response may seem impolite, but she understood that her colleague had bad intentions. If Elena had reacted differently, the person would have given her a list of reasons why they did not like her, which would have made Elena defensive and upset. If the person had approached in a respectful way, Elena would have asked why they did not like her and tried to clear up any misunderstandings.

When faced with a conflict, always keep in mind that a person's character and identity are not defined by a single action, but rather by the sum of all their actions over time. One mistake or misstep does not define a person as a whole. Rather, it is important to consider a person's overall patterns of behavior and the context in which their actions take place in order to truly understand them. It is important to remember that people are complex and multifaceted, and that they have the capacity to change and grow over time. A person's actions should be evaluated in the broader context of their life, rather than as isolated incidents.

What's My Protocol?

As human beings, we often follow routines and habits in our everyday lives. These routines and habits can help us to function efficiently and effectively, and can make our lives easier by reducing the need for us to make decisions about every little thing we do. However, the downside to this is that we can become so accustomed to following these routines and habits that we do so without thinking, almost like we are following a script. In some cases, this can lead us to behave in ways that are not necessarily in our best interests or that are not in line with our values and beliefs.

One way to think about this is to consider how we often follow protocols or rules in different situations, such as at work or in social settings. Just like we follow these protocols without thinking, we can also fall into the habit of following our everyday routines and habits in a similar way. This can be especially dangerous when it comes to our beliefs and values, as we may not even realize that we are being influenced by outside forces or that we are behaving in ways that are not true to ourselves.

It is important for us to make a conscious effort to think for ourselves and to question the rules and routines that we follow.

Life is Finite

One of the key ways in which we can live optimally is by compressing time. This means making the most of the time that we have available to us and not wasting it on activities or pursuits that do not bring us joy or fulfillment. Life is finite, and there is no time to waste on leading one that is mediocre or unfulfilling. Instead, we should strive to fill our lives with friends, activities, and experiences that bring us joy and meaning, and that allow us to make the most of the time we have.

There are several ways in which we can compress time and make the most of our lives. One is to prioritize the things that are most important to us, and to focus our time and energy on these things rather than on less important pursuits. This can help us to avoid becoming bogged down in activities that do not bring us joy or fulfillment, and to ensure that we are making the most of our time.

Another is to eliminate or reduce the amount of time we spend on activities that are not beneficial to us. This can include things like watching TV or scrolling through social media, which can be time-consuming but do not necessarily add value to our lives. By cutting back on these activities, we can free up more time to focus on the things that matter most to us.

Life is a journey, not a destination.— Ralph Waldo Emerson

Life is not about reaching a specific end point or goal, but rather about the journey and experiences we have along the way. We should make the most of the time we have, rather than focusing solely on the end result. This can be a helpful perspective to adopt, as it can help us to appreciate the present moment and to find meaning and purpose in our daily lives.

Passionate Indifference

It's the first minutes of the first karate class, the students line up around a large mat and the instructor calls up an arbitrary member to the center. The instructor proceeds to lightly strike the student in the chest. The result is dramatic—the student flies backwards and ends up on their rear end. The instructor pulls the student back into a standing position, but this time asks the student to bend slightly at the knees and to gently sway back and forth. The strike is repeated; this time the student does not move from their stance but instead gently moves backwards with their upper body and returns to their original position. The lesson learned is that our natural stance is to be rigid in life to face adversity head on—to our detriment. Instead be flexible, absorb the assault, and you will bounce back. We use this true-to-life metaphor to introduce the spiritual warrior's tenet of passionate indifference.

Passionate indifference may seem like an oxymoron, as "passionate" and "indifference" are two words that seem to contradict each other. However, it is possible for someone to be *passionately indifferent* about something, meaning that they are deeply committed to a cause or idea, but are not attached to the outcome of their efforts. This can be an advantageous mindset to have when tackling challenges, as it allows the person to approach the situation with determination and focus regardless of the outcome.

For example, a person who is passionately indifferent about a particular challenge may be fully committed to giving their best effort and working tirelessly to overcome the obstacle.

However, they are also willing to walk away from the situation if it becomes clear that the challenge is not worth it, or if they are not making any progress. This allows them to focus their energy and resources on more productive pursuits, and to avoid becoming overly invested in a situation that is not likely to yield any benefits.

Overall, passionate indifference can be an advantageous mindset to have when tackling challenges. It allows the person to approach the situation with determination and focus, but without becoming overly attached to the outcome. This can help them to avoid becoming overly invested in a situation that is not likely to yield any benefits, and to focus their energy and resources on more productive pursuits.

The Tethers that Bind

Our past experiences can sometimes tether us and prevent us from moving forward and being free. This can happen when we become stuck in negative thought patterns or behaviors that were developed in response to past experiences, and these patterns and behaviors continue to hold us back even though the original experiences are no longer present.

One way to break free from these tethers and move forward is to engage in a process called "recapitulation." This involves revisiting and re-experiencing past experiences in a safe and controlled environment, with the goal of gaining a new perspective on the events and letting go of any negative thoughts or behaviors that may have developed in response to them. By doing this, we can gain a new understanding of the past and free ourselves from its hold on us.

Another approach that can help us move on from our past experiences is cognitive processing therapy (CPT). This type of therapy focuses on helping individuals to change their thought patterns and behaviors in response to past experiences. Through a combination of cognitive and behavioral techniques, CPT can help individuals to develop new ways of thinking and acting that are healthier and more adaptive, and that can help them to move past their past experiences and live more fulfilling lives.

Governing Dynamics

The concept of looking out for both one's own self-interest and the interest of the group is an important one, as it recognizes the interdependent nature of human society. In order to thrive and prosper, this may involve sacrificing a little bit of individual freedom in order to benefit the group.

For example, consider a situation in which a group of people are working together to achieve a common goal. In order for the group to succeed, each individual must contribute their time and effort, and must be willing to sacrifice some of their own freedom in order to support the group's efforts. This might involve things like following certain rules or procedures, or giving up some personal time. By doing this, each individual is able to contribute to the group's success and to achieve their own goals and interests in the process.

The optimal path forward is one that looks out for both the individual and the group. By considering the needs and interests of both parties, we can work together to achieve our goals and to create a better future for everyone. In the long run, this can lead to greater success and fulfillment for both the individual and the group.

Meditation

Meditation is a practice that involves focusing the mind on a particular object, thought, or activity to train attention and awareness. It is often associated with spiritual awakening because it can help to increase self-awareness and understanding, and it can also provide a sense of inner peace and clarity.

During meditation, you may focus on your breath, a mantra, or a visualization, and you may also use other techniques, such as body awareness or loving-kindness meditation. By focusing on these things, you can help to calm the mind and cultivate a sense of stillness and clarity.

As you practice meditation regularly, you may begin to develop a greater understanding of your own thoughts and emotions, and you may also become more aware of the present moment and your surroundings. This increased self-awareness can help to foster a sense of inner peace and understanding, and it can also provide a sense of connection with a higher power or spiritual dimension.

Meditation is not a way of making your mind quiet. It's a way of entering into the quiet that's already there—buried under the 50,000 thoughts the average person thinks every day.—Deepak Chopra

Meditation is not about forcing the mind to be quiet, but rather about finding the quiet that already exists within us. By taking the time to sit in stillness and silence, we can tune out the distractions and noise of the outside world and tap into a deeper sense of peace and clarity within ourselves. Meditation can help to reduce stress, improve focus, and increase self-awareness, making it an important part of a healthy and balanced lifestyle.

On Being Fit

Exercise is important for a spiritual warrior for several reasons. First and foremost, it helps to keep the body healthy and strong, better able to withstand the physical and mental challenges that may arise on the spiritual journey. Exercise can also help to improve mental clarity and focus, which can be valuable tools for a spiritual warrior seeking to understand their own inner nature and connect with a higher power.

Exercise can also have a positive impact on mental and emotional well-being. It can help to reduce stress and anxiety, improve mood, and boost self-confidence, all of which can be important for a spiritual warrior seeking to cultivate inner peace and clarity.

Finally, exercise can be a form of spiritual practice in and of itself. Many spiritual traditions place a strong emphasis on physical discipline and the cultivation of physical strength as a way of cultivating mental and spiritual strength. For a spiritual warrior, exercise can be an opportunity to connect with the body and the present moment, and to develop a sense of discipline and self-control that can be applied to other aspects of life.

Some of the ways that exercise can benefit your health and spiritual well-being include:

- Regular exercise can help to improve your physical health in a number of ways. It can reduce your risk of chronic diseases such as obesity, heart disease, and diabetes, and it can also help to lower blood pressure and improve cholesterol levels. Exercise can also improve your overall fitness level and help you to maintain a healthy weight.
- Regular exercise has been shown to have numerous benefits for mental health. It can reduce stress, anxiety, and depression, and it can also improve your

mood and self-esteem. Exercise can also help to improve your sleep quality and increase your energy levels.

- Studies have shown that regular exercise can help to increase lifespan and reduce the risk of premature death. Exercise can help to strengthen your immune system and improve overall health, which can help you to live a longer, healthier life.
- Exercise has also been shown to improve cognitive function and delay the onset of age-related cognitive decline. It can help to improve memory, concentration, and problem-solving skills, and it can also increase blood flow to the brain, which can help to keep it healthy.

The amount of exercise you need each week will depend on your age, fitness level, and overall health. In general, warriors should engage in at least 150 minutes of moderate-intensity aerobic exercise or 75 minutes of vigorous-intensity aerobic exercise each week. This can be broken down into shorter sessions of at least 10 minutes each.

In addition to aerobic exercise, you should engage in muscle-strengthening activities at least two days per week. This can include activities such as lifting weights, doing push-ups or sit-ups, or using resistance bands.

Learn First, then Teach

It is often the case that people will espouse opinions on a given subject without having any real knowledge or understanding of that subject. This can be frustrating for others who are genuinely interested in learning about the topic, as it can make it difficult to separate fact from opinion and to gain a true understanding of the issue.

One way to address this problem is to follow the principle of "those that know, teach; those that do not, learn." In other words, individuals who are knowledgeable about a given subject should strive to share their knowledge with others, while those who do not have a thorough understanding of the subject should focus on learning as much as they can. This can help to ensure that the information being shared is accurate and well-founded, and that individuals are not simply repeating opinions without any real understanding of the topic.

Additionally, it is important for individuals to avoid trying to teach others until they have learned enough about the subject to do so effectively. This means taking the time to learn as much as possible about a given topic before attempting to share that knowledge with others. By doing this, individuals can avoid spreading misinformation and can instead focus on providing accurate and helpful information to others.

Personal Power

A natural consequence of becoming a spiritual warrior is an increase in your charisma and personal power. Charisma is a personal quality that enables an individual to attract and influence others. It is often described as a certain "je ne sais quoi" or "certain something" that sets someone apart from others and gives them a sense of charm and attractiveness. Personal power refers to the ability to influence and impact others, as well as to achieve your goals and objectives. When you have a strong sense of personal power, you may be perceived as more confident, capable, and charismatic. This often can make you a leader in business or in your personal life. Others will more likely follow your lead and be influenced by you.

However, it's important to remember that with great power comes great responsibility. It's important to use your personal power for the greater good, rather than for selfish or nefarious purposes. Misusing your charisma and personal power can lead to negative consequences for yourself and others.

To avoid unduly influencing people for your own selfish ends, it's important to be mindful of your intentions and to use your personal power ethically and responsibly. This may involve being transparent about your motivations, seeking to understand others' perspectives, and considering the potential impact of your actions on others.

It's also important to recognize that personal power is not an end in itself, but rather a tool that can be used to achieve positive outcomes. By tempering your personal power with empathy, integrity, and a sense of social responsibility, you can use it to make a positive difference in the world.

Barriers of Perception

Reality by Consensus

**Perception and indoctrination define our reality. Both
conspire to ensure you overlook that there is more to our
existence than meets the eye.**

"I saw this young boy on a bike," Robin
Williams once joked in his stand-up act. "He
could do all sorts of tricks with that bike that I

thought were impossible—until the day he learned about gravity." Like many comedic moments, this one highlights events that people don't usually think about or consider deeply. With this casual comment, Robin was pointing out an important truth about life—it is full of mystery and wonder, but our understanding of its possibilities is limited by what is considered socially or culturally acceptable.

Consensus is created through the constant reinforcement of ideas about life that conform to the majority opinion, even though these ideas may not reflect reality. Your view of the world is shaped by the consensus of your family, friends, peers, and other influential figures, whose ideas are often based on insecurity and fear. They may be afraid that others will view the world differently than they do, or that they will be exposed as wrong about their worldview. As social animals, we often seek the approval of others and want to be liked, popular, and part of a group. If we don't conform to external indoctrination, we may fear being ostracized or rejected by our social group.

Many belief systems are just a common language for people seeking meaning in life. From the moment you were born, you have had other people's interpretations of that meaning imposed on you. You are repeatedly told how you must view the world. If you challenge or reject this view, you may hear responses like "no" or "you're wrong." If your ideas differ from those of your peers, you may be reprimanded and pressured to conform until you believe what they believe. In extreme cases, if your worldview is significantly different from others' you may be viewed as radical, in need of therapy, or mentally ill. Deviate even further from the norm, and you may face consequences like being "canceled," labeled as unstable, or possibly even institutionalized.

As social creatures, humans have a natural desire to maintain their social connections. This desire can prevent people from thinking differently from the group for fear of being ostracized. In order to be accepted into the group, people may sacrifice some of their individuality to the will of the collective. However, this acceptance comes at a cost—the loss of individuality.

This fear and insecurity create a barrier to our perception, working together to ensure that we overlook the fact that there is more to our existence than what we can see.

It is unclear whether reality exists on its own, or if it is shaped by the act of observation. We may never know for sure, as our understanding of reality is often limited to our five senses, which are imperfect, and the information that others give us. There are limits to what we can know. To fully understand a system, we would need to exist outside of it. Since we are inside the system, we use perception to try to better understand our reality. Perception refers to the processes that help us make sense of different stimuli. Our perceptions are based on how we interpret various sensations, but our senses are not always reliable. For example, light can affect our eyesight, the image on the back of our retinas is upside down, and our brain tries to fill in any missing information. The brain also combines other sensory input, like emotional context from the vagus nerve, to complete our interpretation or "description" of the current moment. This interpretation is influenced not only by our senses, but also by our past experiences, past indoctrination, and current emotional state. To maintain continuity, the brain actually converges on an interpretation that is about 15 seconds in the past, rather than in real-time. The final result is often unclear and subjective.

What we "see" is just a small portion of what objective reality has to offer. What would happen if we allowed ourselves to consider the possibility that there is more to our existence than what we can perceive with our senses? There is a vast world of possibilities beyond our senses that many people never consider, but anyone can access it if they choose.

Once we become aware of the limitations that bind us, we must work to understand reality, or else we will be at the mercy of the current, like a leaf on a river. Many people have accepted this fate, giving up the effort to challenge relentless indoctrination and accepting what they are told about the world. They become like a "brick in the wall," a cookie-cutter version of their family, friends, and peers. While some people may try to stand out by adding a little glitter, underneath it all, their view of existence is largely the same as those around them.

Lazy by Design

Why do humans tend to be receptive to indoctrination? One reason is that we are naturally lazy and our bodies try to conserve energy whenever possible. Thinking critically about reality at every step requires effort and a conscious expenditure of energy, and few people are willing to make that effort. Our bodies may also resist this effort. Fear is also a factor—we want to be accepted by our family and friends, and if we challenge their worldview, we risk being rejected, ridiculed, and potentially isolated.

There are two modes of thought: "System 1" is fast, instinctive, and emotional, while "System 2" is slower, more deliberate, and more logical. System 2 requires more energy and generates more heat, and the body resists using it. This is why people are often quick to adopt "reality by consensus"—it is easier to accept what others tell us rather than critically evaluating each alternative. This tendency to rely on System 1 could explain why memes spread rapidly in our society. They are often slick, packaged ideas that are readily accepted and rarely challenged, and people pass them on to their social circle without realizing it.

> Albert Einstein viewed the intuitive mind as a sacred gift and the rational mind as a faithful servant.

If you want to remain lazy, go with the flow, and be a leaf on a river, you may have more friends and life may be easier in some ways. However, if you want to overcome self-ignorance and strive for enlightenment, you will need to become a "spiritual warrior." This will require you to make strategic decisions and take the time to better understand the mysteries of life, challenging your own assumptions about the world. Don't simply accept what others tell you—instead, consider which beliefs you have accepted because you were told them, and which ones you should continue to hold onto after critically examining them. The beliefs that you retain will define you as a unique individual.

We all seek happiness, and to a spiritual warrior, happiness is achieved by adhering to a consistent set of basic beliefs in life. You should start by establishing a few axioms, which are beliefs that you have faith in because you cannot prove them. After you have a small set of axioms, you can include a limited number of tenets—beliefs that you have thought about and decided have value to you. For example, you might adopt the tenet that in any given situation, you should always give more than you take.

Each tenet should be independent of the others. In other words, no two tenets should be variations on the same theme—each should be unique. If these tenets are consistent with each other and you remain faithful to them, you will likely experience happiness. However, don't stop there—aim for exuberance. If your beliefs contradict each other or you waver in your adherence to them, you will inevitably experience disharmony, cognitive dissonance, and ultimately, unhappiness in life.

Having a clear set of basic beliefs can make decision-making easier. Each decision should align with one of your tenets. This will make you more self-reliant and give you more control over your life and surroundings. Instead of drifting aimlessly, you will be living deliberately. As a result, you will experience less fear and conflict. The goal is to let go of your defenses and current understandings of reality, and allow yourself to see the world in a new way, based on your refined set of tenets.

Changing your worldview changes the way you see the world. This openness to the world around you will allow you to experience aspects of reality that may have previously escaped you. These "non-ordinary" aspects of reality are available for anyone to explore. To access these dimensions, you must connect with the "energetic being" within you, which most people are only vaguely aware of, if at all.

The Philosophy of Self

Most people think of their "self" as their physical being—their identity, senses, emotions, and perception of the world. This view is self-centered and narcissistic, assuming that the individual is the center of the universe, and it can be quite limiting.

The spiritual self enables you to see beyond yourself and connect with other people and the world. Empathy allows us to understand others and have a more objective view of ourselves and our surroundings. By trying to see the world from another person's perspective, we can gain insight into their experiences and have a more rounded understanding of the world.

Many people are aware of their physical and spiritual selves, but may not realize that there is a third aspect of the self—the energetic being. This energy radiates from your body and surrounds you, and is present in all living and nonliving things. Each individual has a unique energy signature that distinguishes them from others.

Have you ever felt instantly drawn to someone you just met, or comfortable sitting on a rock? This may be because your energy signature is resonating with that person or object. On the other hand, if you find a new acquaintance annoying or a new location anxiety-inducing, it may be because their energy is not compatible with yours and being around them could make you miserable. In this case, it is best to remove yourself from the situation as quickly as possible.

The tentacles of energy fragments emanating from your body fluctuate, similar to the energy radiating from the sun. These energy fragments typically create an aura that extends just under an inch from your body and surrounds it completely. Some people have auras that extend several inches, while others can radiate their energy for several feet. Some people can also create a sudden burst of energy, like a solar flare. These phenomena can be observed in the non-ordinary reality discussed below.

Your energetic being exists, but is often undiscovered or ignored. This energy serves as a connection to part of reality that can be overlooked. It is a way to break down the barriers of perception and access non-ordinary reality. This expanded view of the world may be surprising and even intimidating at first, but once you understand how it works, the awe and fear will fade and you can incorporate this new perspective into your daily life. By touching the energy emitted by other people and objects, you can gain direct knowledge that bypasses your usual intuitive or cognitive thinking.

Non-Ordinary Reality

Non-ordinary reality refers to events that may be perceived as strange or unusual by a hypothetical person who holds a limited view of the world. This could include things like accurately predicting the future or seeing someone disappear before your eyes. These types of events are often dismissed as coincidences or hallucinations, but if you are open to the possibility of non-ordinary reality and able to overcome fear, it may become a regular part of your experience.

Arthur C. Clarke, a science fiction author, once said that any technology that is advanced enough may appear like magic to those who don't understand it. In other words, as people come to understand and accept new technologies, they may no longer be seen as extraordinary or mysterious. The same is true for non-ordinary reality, or events and experiences that are outside of what is considered normal or expected by most people. At first, these experiences may seem like coincidences, delusions, or pseudo-science, but as people become more receptive and open-minded, they may come to see them as a part of their daily lives.

Hamlet says that there are more things in the universe than what we can imagine or understand. I have personally experienced some of these extraordinary events that go beyond our everyday understanding of reality. These experiences are not limited to me alone; anyone can access this expanded view of reality if they are open to it and let go of their preconceived notions and fears. By rejecting the limitations of social conditioning and embracing curiosity and openness, we can discover the endless wonders of the universe that lie beyond our ordinary perceptions.

Spidey Sense

Sometimes I experience a strong intuition or gut feeling about future events, similar to the 'spidey sense' described in the Spider-Man comics. This 'sixth sense' allows me to sense potential danger or other important information with a high level of accuracy and certainty.

> the distinction between past, present and future is only a stubbornly persistent illusion— Albert Einstein

My Spidey sense allows me to sense danger and accurately predict the future. This is different from intuition, which is just a feeling about a situation. My Spidey sense has never been wrong in its predictions. Some of my friends ask me for guidance using my Spidey sense, but it doesn't work like that. I can't control when I receive these flashes of knowledge, and they simply pop into my head without warning. Some scientists believe that time is not linear, which could mean that my predictions are actually memories of events that have already happened.

I had a moment of insight while watching the State of the Union address with a friend. A sudden thought popped into my head that someone would stand up and shout from the balcony during the speech. To my surprise, this prediction came true when the father of a high school student killed in a shooting was removed from the audience after shouting from the balcony during the speech. While some may view this as a simple coincidence, I have found that my intuitive flashes like this are always accurate.

Magical Deer

As I was leaving my mother's house after a visit with her and my cousin, I turned to say goodbye and hesitated before saying, "See you, Mum." I had a sudden feeling that something was not quite right.

Mum asked, "What's up?"

As I left my mother's house, I told her goodbye and started walking towards my home. Suddenly, I had a feeling that I would encounter a deer on my way. I knew I had to be cautious and make sure not to hit it. My mother was familiar with my premonitions, as she had witnessed them many times before. However, my cousin was more skeptical and didn't believe in such things.

Despite their different reactions, my prediction came true. As I neared my home at the top of a hill, I remembered the deer and slowed down. Sure enough, a six-point buck appeared on the road just a foot in front of my car. It looked at me and then calmly crossed to the other side, out of harm's way.

Did I use my intuition or some kind of sixth sense to avoid a potentially dangerous situation on the road with a deer, or was it the deer itself that communicated with me through some kind of energy to avoid the collision? Either way, I was able to avoid any potential harm or damage to myself or the animal.

Tree Fall Down

I recently experienced a hurricane with wind speeds of 100 mph and heavy rain from the safety of my porch. As I looked at the trees in my neighbor's backyard, I noticed one tree that seemed like it was going to fall. But it didn't. A week later, another intense storm hit and the power went out. I went to a friend's house to shower and as I drove behind my neighbor's home, I saw that the road was blocked by the same tree that I had thought would fall.

Death Makes Itself Known

My mother had a long history of smoking, which led to a number of health issues including COPD and emphysema. Despite receiving oxygen treatment, the doctors gave her only a year to live. Five years later, I was visiting her and trying to figure out how to keep her at home instead of in a nursing home. I lived too far away to provide much direct assistance, but I had a friend who was unemployed and lived nearby. I thought about offering him some money to help with tasks like grocery shopping and banking for my mother, in an effort to help her stay in her apartment longer.

I had a feeling that my mother's health was going to take a turn for the worse, and that my friend's help in taking care of her would not be needed. When I arrived at my mother's home, I was overwhelmed with emotion and told her that I believed she was going to die soon. Instead of dismissing my statement, my mother took it seriously and called her sister to come and visit. Sure enough, a week and a half later, my mother passed away. My past experiences with accurate premonitions had led my mother to trust my intuition and make preparations for her death.

Disappear From the Face of the Earth

In the midst of the daily hustle and bustle, it can be refreshing to take a break and escape into nature. Imagine floating down a river on a sunny day, the warm sun shining down and not a cloud in sight. It's a simple yet enjoyable way to relax and unwind from the responsibilities and stress of everyday life.

Lexy and I were still in the early stages of getting to know each other when we decided to spend a leisurely day floating down the river near our homes. As the sun shone brightly and there were no clouds in the sky, we enjoyed the peaceful and serene atmosphere. After a few hours, we decided to head to the riverbank. We were surprised to find that there was no one in sight and the area was surrounded by trees, a field of grass, and rows of corn rising up a hill.

As Lexy and I left the river and stepped onto the riverbank, the weather changed dramatically.

Dark clouds rolled in quickly, seeming to hang just above us. The sun was blocked out and it became almost twilight-dark. The winds picked up, making it necessary to shout to be heard. It felt like the clouds and winds were pressing against me, and there was a buzzing in my ear.

Lexy began to panic, shouting and reaching out blindly as if she couldn't see or hear me even though I was standing right next to her. She became overwhelmed with fear and started crying. It was a scary and confusing experience for both of us.

Just as suddenly as it had started, the strange weather passed and everything returned to normal. She looked at me and asked, "Where did you go? Why did you leave me?" Lexy was so scared by the experience that she refused to talk about it again.

Ghosts can be so Mischievous

I visited Lexy at her home and she told me about the old house she had purchased. It came with all the usual features like hardwood floors, a dishwasher, and two bathrooms, but it also came with a ghost. Lexy said the ghost was an old woman who used to be the owner of the house. As we walked through the house, Lexy showed me each room except for one that was off limits because that's where the ghost was said to reside. As we made our way back to the first floor, we noticed that all the lights that had been on were now off. It seemed like the ghost was trying to make her presence known.

As I left Lexy's house on my motorcycle, I discovered that the lights weren't working. No matter how many times I tried flipping the switch, they still didn't turn on. I couldn't help but wonder if the ghost that Lexy had told me about was somehow responsible. Despite the lack of lighting, I decided to ride through the city streets anyway. I couldn't let a ghost deter me from leaving.

I occasionally tried the switch to see if the lights would come on. When I reached the highway, I became concerned about the danger of riding at night without lights. But as I worried, the lights suddenly turned on and I had no further issues with the motorcycle's lights.

I Know What You're Thinking

Sometimes, my energetic being produces a burst of energy that originates in my gut and searches for a similar burst from someone else. When these two bursts connect, I am able to access the other person's thoughts through a "direct knowledge" stream. I may say things about them that we have never discussed before, things that I couldn't possibly have known. In some cases, this energetic connection can last for hours, but others may be frightened by it and break the connection after a few minutes.

Non-ordinary reality experiences, such as mind reading or energy connection, can be unsettling for those who encounter them. In my experience, I have initiated these connections with others, but in one instance, someone else initiated the connection with me and tried to drain my energy. To protect myself, I ended the connection and told the person to leave. When they shared the experience with others, they were met with disbelief and doubt. However, finding just one person who can validate the experience can help bring a sense of understanding and normalcy. It's important to remember that these types of experiences, while unusual, are not uncommon and can be a source of wonder and exploration.

The following day, the person who initiated the energy connection wanted to learn more about the energetic being. However, since they had accessed it without any prior experience, I felt it was best to let it go. They were not ready to fully experience the wonders of non-ordinary reality. It is important to be prepared and have some understanding of the energetic being before attempting to access it.

Light up the Room

The energetic being can also manifest in a way that causes two or more people to "light up a room." This does not mean that their auras literally emit light, but rather that the energy from multiple individuals combine and expand to fill the entire room. This can be a very enjoyable experience if you are with the right person, as the energy that surrounds you can feel serene and protective, almost like being back in the womb.

During this state, you may feel free of doubt, insecurity, and worries.

Sophie is a massage therapist who has experienced the phenomenon of "lighting up a room" with other therapists. This occurs during sessions when both people are relaxed and fully present in the moment, allowing the flow of energy between them to grow and expand, filling the entire room. This energy can be visualized as a fusion of colors and is characterized by a feeling of peace and serenity. Sophie has also mentioned that groups of therapists have been known to "light up a room" together, using massage as a way to facilitate this experience.

I am not afraid of these unusual occurrences. I view them as real as getting up in the morning to make breakfast. However, the scientific side of me likes to explore the limits of these events. One time, Sophie was sitting in the lotus position with her eyes closed, allowing the energy to flow. I approached her and tried to move my hands in front of her body, but there was an invisible force preventing me from touching her. No matter how hard I pushed, my hands couldn't get within a foot of her. She was completely unaware of my attempt to enter her space. I was fascinated by this experience, but I let it go. After all, it's a non-ordinary reality, and it seems that anything is possible. Just relax and enjoy.

You're Pregnant

My partner stepped off the plane after a two-week vacation. "You're pregnant," I said. News to her, but confirmed within a few days.

"Sorry I had to reschedule our appointment," my hairdresser said to me.

"Did you have a doctor's appointment about your baby?" I responded.

With a look of bewilderment on her face, she said, "How did you know? I haven't even told my friends yet."

It is possible that the body undergoes subtle changes at the start of pregnancy, and it could be that I am simply more perceptive than others. However, my belief is that the energetic being within us all radiates energy that some individuals are able to detect and interpret. Pregnancy is easy to spot in this way, as instead of noticeable physical changes in the woman's body, there are subtle shifts in her energy.

Medical Intuition

"Remember how I told you I've been getting a pain in my stomach? Well, a couple of days ago I bent over in pain on the elevator. I couldn't get up off the floor. I saw a doctor and he has scheduled me for gallbladder surgery next week," Dylan told me over the phone.

"Dylan, it's not your gallbladder. There's something wrong with your lower spine."

What do I know? Dylan lives hours from me, and I hadn't seen him in a year. And now I'm giving him medical advice remotely without the benefit of a medical degree or a CT scan.

Dylan was a close friend of mine who had witnessed my 'Spidey sense' on multiple occasions. So when I called him with a gut feeling that something was wrong with his health, he took it seriously and began frantically trying to schedule a second opinion. He was able to secure an appointment with a doctor going on vacation the following week, who, upon examining him and getting a scan, discovered that Dylan had a tumor wrapped around his lower spine. Without surgery within a month, the doctor said Dylan would likely be paralyzed for life. Fortunately, he was able to have the surgery and make a full recovery.

Manifest Destiny

Our energetic being has the ability to connect with both living and nonliving things in the universe which radiate energy. By manipulating this energy, we can influence our environment and bring about a desired outcome through the process of manifestation. This can be as simple as praying for a specific result or actively directing energy towards a particular goal. While this may seem unconventional, many people have experienced the power of manifestation through prayer or other intentional practices.

The concept of manifesting involves manipulating energy in order to bring about a desired outcome. This can be done through prayer or intention. In my experience, when I manifest something, I feel a click that signals to me that the event I have manifested will definitely come true. I have used this technique to manifest things like the gender of my child, financial resources when needed, and even good weather on a day when rain was predicted. While some may see this as pseudo-science, I have found that it can be a powerful tool for creating positive change in my life.

I am cautious in my use of manifesting, as manipulating energy can be draining for me. Additionally, I understand that the manifestation of certain events may have consequences for others, as in the case of manifesting a new job which could potentially deprive someone else of the opportunity. Therefore, I try to be mindful of my intentions and use manifesting sparingly, leaving room for others to have their own experiences in the world.

Divenire

Paradise Found

No one could have imagined that a simple trip to reconnect with a friend would instead unravel the mysteries of life and our very existence.

It had been five years since Christian last saw Ilsa.

Christian instructed the driver to drop him off at the beach, much to the driver's disbelief. "It's quite a distance from any hotel," the driver pointed out. Christian simply replied, "I have a friend meeting me there. They have a car and will take me to the hotel afterwards. Thanks for the ride."

The driver just shrugged.

Ilsa had always had an affinity for the ocean, so much so that after all these years apart, she wanted to meet him in Bodega Cove rather than her new home.

Ilsa and Christian had a deep connection that went beyond the physical. They would often spend hours discussing spiritual topics and delving into each other's thoughts. They would take walks in parks and woods and sometimes hold each other for hours. While they did have a sexual relationship, it was not a main focus for them. Eventually, Ilsa moved away for a new job and they lost touch, occasionally seeing each other when they could over the years. They both went on to have other partners and marriages, but their bond remained strong despite the distance and changes in their lives.

The beach was located down a flight of steps from the highway, over a hill. To the north, the foot of a steep mountain could be seen breaking across the sand, creating a rocky promontory extending into the water. The trees on the mountain slopes were showing the autumnal colors of fall. To the south, the beach faded into a hazy distance.

The sand was deserted, as one would expect on a late October weekday. However, he saw her green towel with a large, colorful parrot on it, just as she had promised. Ilsa had mentioned on the phone that she would likely go for a run up to the point before he arrived and he could find her there if he wished.

He left his things by her towel and ran.

Although the sun was shining and the weather was relatively warm for a fall day with a breeze, there was no one else in sight along the beach all the way to the promontory. There were footprints, however—Ilsa's, slightly blown about by the wind, leading out but not yet returning.

The tracks led to a narrow cave in the rocky outcrop, just above the tide line. He thought it wouldn't hurt to take a look and see if the opening extended all the way through like a tunnel, potentially finding Ilsa resting in the cove on the other side.

As he ventured deeper into the cave, it became darker and narrower. He could no longer see Ilsa's tracks or much of anything else. He was just about to turn back when his foot slipped and he fell into a hole in the ground. His head struck a rock and everything went black.

When Christian came to, he had difficulty remembering where he was or how he got there.

The cave seemed bigger and brighter than before, and he wondered if it actually opened out to the other side of the point, with just a drop between two different levels. He was lying on his back in a few inches of water, but there was no evidence of blood and, to his surprise, he couldn't find any injuries. He struggled to his feet, his legs feeling stiff but stable, and followed the light up and out.

As he neared the cave opening, he automatically reached for his phone, but it was not in its usual pocket. After searching all of his pockets, he couldn't find it anywhere. He assumed it must have fallen out during his fall.

The cave opening was wide and tall. To his left rose the mountain—or was it even the same mountain?—but the ridge behind the cave seemed higher on this side, blocking any view of the ocean. He had to follow the cleft uphill. He could hear birds chirping and the faint sound of running water, possibly from a nearby stream. The sun was bright and unusually warm.

The trail gently descended, surrounded by blue, yellow, and purple flowers, before emerging from a line of trees and leading to a stone bridge over a river gorge. The wooden roof of the bridge was carved to let sunbeams dapple the span in a checkerboard pattern of shadow and light.

At the head of the bridge stood a tall and muscular woman, gazing away from it. She was dressed in a burnt orange dress that reached the top of her leather shoes, her long jet black hair flowing in the wind. The dress was fitted at her waist, secured with a wide brown belt. In her right hand was a long staff that appeared to be made of glass, with a broad rounded crescent at the top. The tip of the staff glistened in the sunlight, casting a rainbow on the bridge floor as if it were a prism.

"Hello, miss, can you help me?" he called out as he approached. "I bumped my head and I think I'm lost."

Nothing. There was no reaction from the woman. He stepped around in front of her to capture her attention. "Hi, I need your help. I'm lost and I think I may be injured."

She continued to stare straight ahead and without a word, she lifted her staff and pointed the crescent toward the other side of the bridge.

"I could really use your help, lady," he said more forcefully.

Once again silence, and with a small flick of the staff, she motioned once again for Christian to cross.

California, he figured. At least she didn't seem dangerous.

The trail on the far side of the bridge ran down through a field of purple, yellow, and blue flowers to a crystal clear lake surrounded by mountains that stretched to the horizon. There was no indication of the highway. However, there was a sailboat anchored in the shallow waters, with two men nearby and what appeared to be a woman lounging on the deck.

As he approached the sailboat, he shouted out, "Hi, I sure could use your help."

"Certainly," one of the men responded as they both turned toward Christian "How can we be of service?"

"Hi. My name is Christian. I'm a bit confused. I came to visit my friend and was looking for her on the beach and…" He recounted the series of events that had led him here.

"Oh, that's Nola. She doesn't talk. That's not her purpose," the second man said.

"I'm Alexander," said the first. "That's Stephane, and over there is Olivia."

The woman glanced at Christian, then turned her face back to the sun and closed her eyes again.

"Forgive me, but where am I?"

"You're in Divenire," Alexander replied.

"Never heard of it. I was on the beach in Bodega Cove."

"Can't say I know it." Stephane looked at Alexander and cracked a smile.

"Then how did I get here? How far is it from the beach?"

"Well I can't help you there, Christian. This is Divenire. That's all I know."

Alexander interjected, "Christian, it looks like you've been through a lot. Let me get you some food. We have wine as well. We can try to answer your questions as best we can."

This had to be a cult. He must have wandered to the wrong side of the point and stumbled upon a cult compound. Christian had read about these types of situations. He wondered if Ilsa had also fallen victim to these people—or if she was already a member and this whole plan was to get him to join.

Best not show any of that, though. "Sure," he said, "I'd love some wine, but one question first, if you don't mind. I told you I was looking for my friend. Her name is Ilsa and she's about five-seven, blonde…"

Olivia suddenly sat up. "Ilsa! I loved her. She visited with us a bit ago. She's fine. Have something to settle you and I'll tell you how to get to Isabella and Sophia's place. She went to visit with them. How lucky you are, she's sweet."

Stephane went below to retrieve some wine and bread while Christian joined them on the deck, still wary but trying not to show it.

"So how do you know each other?" he asked.

"We're from here," said Olivia.

"You have homes on the lake?"

"No, we live on the sloop."

"Well how do you know each other?"

"We met and just hit it off."

"What do you all do for a living?"

"Do you mean work? We don't work, we just enjoy sailing on the lake and soaking up the sun."

"But what did you do before you decided to… throw it all away?" Christian asked, choosing his words carefully.

Alexander said, "Some time ago I was an accountant. Olivia was a webcam girl. Stephane was a bodyguard for CEOs, quite well known and sought after. But that was a long time ago. We never think of it any more. We live in the moment now and just enjoy life."

Despite further questioning, the most Christian could learn from the people on the boat was that Ilsa was at a cottage about a mile from the lake. "You can't miss it. It's bright pink; there's nothing else like it in Divenire," they said. They didn't mention belonging to a group, but Stephane did speak excitedly about "Simpson," who often met with visitors and was presumably the cult leader.

The path wound around the blue of the lakeshore. He could see fish darting just below the water's surface, and the breeze gently brushed against his neck. There were more flowers here, the same as near the bridge, and the smaller trees up ahead were still in bloom. How was this possible in October, he wondered. There was even a hint of lilacs in the air.

Despite the oddity of the situation and the strange residents of Divenire, Christian found himself relaxing in the unseasonably warm and fragrant air. Work felt very far away. The cottage was exactly as described—bright pink and situated behind a stand of trees, off the path. It was a single-story building, about twenty-five feet wide and deep. The windows were open, with a potted flower on each sill.

He could hear voices coming from the back of the cottage, where Christian discovered a stone patio with a tall, wide rock wall that was comfortable to sit on. Beyond the patio was a flagstone path leading to a garden in the back, where rectangular and circular beds grew various plants—tomatoes in one bed, corn in another, and peppers in another. Some areas had flowers, while others were bare and raked as if they were being prepared for new seedlings. In the center stood a pergola covered in blooming lilacs.

Three women were crouched down, working in one of the beds, accompanied by a small dog that barked and ran towards Christian. At the noise, one of the women turned around and exclaimed with delight, "Christian, you're here!" and rushed towards him.

Ilsa flung her arms around him and hugged him as closely as two humans can get. Then she turned and pulled him toward the other two, saying, "I can't believe you're here too. What a surprise. Come meet my friends. Sophia, this is Christian. Christian meet Isabella."

Both looked harmless, if a little New Age in their hair and clothes, and seemed older than Ilsa and him. Isabella spoke first. "Ilsa's told us all about you. In truth, I thought you'd be taller."

Sophia laughed. "Not as geeky as I'd expected, though."

"Nice to meet you," he said. "Is it okay if I talk with Ilsa alone for a moment?"

Ilsa shook her head. "Christian, they're fine. Whatever you say to me, they can hear as well."

There was nothing in her eyes to suggest she was one of them, but he wasn't wholly sure. "Fair enough, maybe Isabella and Sophia can help. I had some questions about this place and how I got here. And more importantly, how can we get—"

"Christian," Isabella interrupted, "I can understand why you'd be impatient, but there's no need to be hasty. Simpson is the caretaker of this place. He can provide answers to any question you have. That's his purpose. We promise. Let me show you our garden before you go."

Ilsa took Christian's hand and they followed Isabella and Sophia around the growing plots, taking turns to describe each in great detail until they came to the last and a wistful look came over Isabella.

"I planted this dwarf cherry when I arrived here," she said looking at the spindly tree heavy with blossoms in front of them. "Not much different from you, in some ways. I'd like to think someone, maybe Ilsa or yourself, would look after the garden when Sophia and I eventually leave."

"So people do leave?" Christian seized on her words. "Can we just get out of this… compound or whatever it is?"

"You should talk to Simpson now. There's a skiff drawn up on the beach below us."

They made their way down to the water. From the beach, Isabella pointed to a building made completely of glass that rose from the mountainside across the lake, surrounded by trees. "That's where you should go," she told him. "He'll explain everything."

The skiff was long and narrow. It reminded him of the boats he had seen in documentaries about Vietnam. The thin paddle laid across its seats had the same crescent symbol he'd seen on the staff of the woman on the bridge, Nola.

"If you want me to help with the garden, I could stay," Ilsa said, but the two women just shook their heads.

"You know you need to go with him. That's your purpose right now," Sophia replied. "We'll be here when you come back."

Christian hauled the boat out into the shallows and helped Ilsa aboard. It was surprisingly easy to paddle. Behind, he heard Isabella call out, "See you two soon," as the women turned away to return to their gardening.

Not wanting to upset them or Ilsa, he murmured to himself, "Hopefully not."

He had a hundred questions he wanted to ask now that they were alone—why they were there, how to get out, who these people were. But

before he could speak, Ilsa reached out and
gently took the paddle from his hands, placing it
in the bottom of the boat to let them drift. She
looked deeply into his eyes as she slowly sat in
his lap and kissed him like she was savoring the
sun.

"We've got all the time we need," she
murmured. "And it's been so long."

She removed her bralette and pulled her skirt to
the side, while Christian quickly undressed, the
intensity between them growing. He gently
entered her.

Afterwards, he lay with his eyes closed and
counted his blessings. He was with Ilsa, nestled
in the crook of his arm, under the sun with not a
cloud in the sky. Despite being knocked
unconscious and getting lost in a cult compound,

it was a glorious day. He reflected that things could be much worse.

Ilsa woke him when the skiff's hull scraped against the far shore. "Christian, we're here," she whispered.

He opened his eyes and said, "Maybe all's right with the world after all."

"We can keep it that way."

After a moment, she pointed to the hill just off the shore and the glass building they had seen from the other side. As they walked up the narrow path towards it, Christian could see directly inside. It wasn't a house so much as a single room, in the center of which sat an old man gently rocking back and forth in a chair. He had long white hair, deeply tanned skin, and a blank expression on his face.

A door slid open to admit them and the old man, who Christian assumed was Simpson, gestured at the floor smoothly, with no sign of age or stiffness.

"Sit right there," he said.

"Mr. Simpson, I'd like—"

"I know what you would like."

"You know, I wish just once someone here would let me finish a sentence."

"Well, we do have all the time in the world, so I could patiently listen to your stories of misfortune, but why? I'm the caretaker of Divenire. It's my job to know everyone here.

Christian, you want to know how you got here, what this place is, and how you can leave"

There was that "purpose" nonsense again. "That's right, I do."

"As I said, I know. First, there is only one way out of Divenire. And that cave you came from is not it. That was just your way in."

"That's crazy."

Ilsa touched him on the arm. "It's not, Christian. It's true."

"There are people here. They have food, homes, and lives. How did they get in?"

Simpson sighed. "All in their own ways. They come past Nola to Divenire, just like you after your fall in the cave. She's the guardian. That's her purpose."

"And you keep everyone here once they get here?"

"Do you feel trapped? Has anyone trapped you?"

"I…" Christian stopped. "I don't know."

"Go to the bridge and see Nola with Ilsa. Then decide for yourself. I promise you, you won't be able to return the way you came, but I can't explain why. You'll have to understand it on your own. You need to so that your time will come. Ilsa understands better than you do."

With that, Simpson went back to rocking in his chair and the door behind them slid open again suggesting he was being dismissed. "Do you?"

Christian whispered to her as they left the house again.

"I remember the cave," she said, linking her arm through his. "I remember what happened to me there. Better than you do."

They walked around the far side of the lake. There were many paths, but each either led back to the water or ended at a rock formation, cliff, or ravine. Eventually, though, they entered the field of flowers and Christian knew the bridge was just a short distance ahead. The sun was still high in the sky, though his arrival felt like it had been many hours ago.

Nola stood at the far end of the bridge, just as she had when he first crossed, her staff still in her hand. He edged out onto the span, moving Ilsa behind him for her safety. Nola didn't move.

"What is this place?" he said. "Simpson said you'd show us."

Nola said nothing. When Christian stepped forward, she stamped the end of her staff on the ground and declared, "None may pass this way." He noticed that she could talk after all. Then, her staff lit up with a brightness akin to the sun and she looked up into the sky.

As Christian had experienced since moving to Divenire, the sky was always impeccably clear. However, in the direction that Nola was gazing, a cloud seemed to suddenly appear and rise above them. Upon its completion, the cloud displayed an image of a woman in a delivery room, with a nurse observing as a midwife in scrubs held a newborn baby that had just emerged from the woman's body. The infant could be heard crying as it inhaled its first breaths of air.

He heard Simpson's voice roll from above. "This is for each of you, to be born again."

As Christian pieced everything together, he realized that the cave, the fall, and Ilsa's comments about him remembering more than he initially thought all made sense. It was peculiar to consider that they likely passed away close together in time. He pondered what the person who discovered their corpses would make of the situation.

And he found he felt no sadness at all. He already knew what came next, where he was, what his existence in Divenire would be.

Ilsa slipped her hand in his. "You knew already," he said.

"I remembered a lot more of what happened to me, and I worked it out much faster. They told me everyone needs to come to terms with Divenire in their own time. Are you okay?"

He smiled at her. "I couldn't be better. This place couldn't be better. Let's go swimming. Afterwards, I want to plant some sunflowers in Isabella's and Sophia's garden."

The Awakening

For the last few years she'd lived at a low intensity and built an inner world to which no one could come—until she met him.

Solitude

Anna sits on the floor with her legs spread wide as she sorts through a stack of papers in front of her. The sun is just beginning to rise, casting beams of white and yellow light into the room through the windows. Anna is still wearing her nightgown, a white and sheer garment that glows in the sunlight. She looks relaxed and peaceful as she works.

She is alone, with no plans or appointments for the day. She takes slow, deliberate sips of her coffee, savoring the quiet moment to herself. There is no need to rush today, no one depending on her or demanding her attention. She can simply sit and enjoy the peaceful solitude.

Pinning up her hair, she thinks she hears a noise, and she sits attentively and cocks her head, listening intently. The only noise she can discern is the ever-present sound of the street below. Cars speeding away from red lights or honking, people greeting each other over the din are all too familiar, and she has over time learned to ignore it.

There it is again. Not in the street, but right there in her apartment. In her hallway behind her. The muted sound of footsteps approaching. How can this be? She lives alone, single, free of attachments, with plenty of acquaintances but few friends. She has never been one to ask people to her apartment, save for her friends, and this is an intruder.

Her first instinct is to turn around and face them—but she doesn't. There is no malevolence in the footsteps. Their gentleness signals there is no danger, that this person will not harm her. She's filled with euphoria and panic at the same time. It must be him, she thinks. But how? They've never met other than the occasional video chat with her spiritual meet-up group.

His name is Christian; last names aren't permitted in the group chat. She hasn't even seen his face. She reveals herself to the camera, but he does not, only his voice is known to her. They talked of philosophical and spiritual matters, both intrigued by the scope of each other's reading and the depth and quality of their minds. Yet there was an energy on a level beneath that conversation, their minds and spirits touching even with the substantial distance separating them. After many hours of chatting with Christian over the days and weeks, she had been touched by his patience, kindness, sensuality and respect. Anna has tried to think of the right words for everything she feels about him, but some have probably not been invented yet.

She could never have imagined herself in a cyber romance. It's far from real but certainly doesn't feel that way. She felt the same as she has in past romances, the intense feelings of tenderness, elation, of closeness, and even the occasional disappointment. She enjoys her free time and living alone. But at the same time, Anna is grateful to be touched by a soul who lives more in their own interior world and can understand her beyond words and without physical touch. It hurts when she thinks that in reality it will remain at this distance.

Anna let herself be driven by his energy. She would love to feel his hands embracing her from behind, but every chord of his that touches her has the same effect, and she feels protected, but also free and encouraged to feel.

She imagines Christian on a precipice, facing an approaching storm, clothes clinging to his body under the force of the wind. But the storm is no match for his power within. He is stronger, more confident, more capable of realizing all of his potential all at once.

When she chats with Christian, she enjoys knowing he looks longingly upon her face and her body. He often asks her to reveal herself to him, and she does, and she relishes his sighs when he realizes he can see but cannot touch, cannot smell that scent that is uniquely hers. She enjoys this power she has over him. But now it's his turn. He has found his way to her.

But wait! He's a gentle soul, but it can't be him, he's a world away. Thousands of miles separate them. She starts to turn, but it's too late. He is behind her, his legs parallel hers and his body pressed against her back. Christian's hands hold her face forward to prevent her from turning, but gently. Just enough to tell her she is safe, and that it is him and now he is in command. He wants her to surrender to him. Now that he is here in her apartment, she doesn't care that she feels naked, as if her life and all her secrets are laid at his feet.

How can this be? She feels his warm breath on the back of her neck. It's an inviting warmth and her body stirs in response. A stirring she has not felt for some time, if ever. The exquisite feeling starts at her neck and spreads to her breasts and down to her root chakra. As Christian holds her, it is as if he is holding on for the life inside them. No words are exchanged. Wait, it can't be him? It's not possible.

He suddenly kisses her. It is a tentative, innocent pressing of the lips. She understands at once that in accepting and returning that innocent touch she has crossed a boundary, she has passed through a turnstile from which there is no way back. Nothing in her life will ever be quite the same. And, realizing it too, grasping the weight of her feelings, he quietly laughs.

He moves his hands along the sides of her body. She melts, no longer in control. Her gown is thin and she can feel every micro-movement. She can feel his muscles, his strength, as his arms press against her. Muscles that do not come from his job sitting at a desk and typing. His hands lightly touch the sides of her breasts, and she gasps. Anna wants more than anything to feel the uncompromising sexuality that washes over her as she presses herself against him. This is the proverbial decisive moment, both spontaneous and ephemeral. In the past, she let the moment pass and it was lost never to be found again. Not this time. Anna gives herself permission to succumb, and she embraces him with all of her being.

Her breathing quickens as his right hand moves across her stomach, then along the top of her legs as his breath continues to lie upon her neck, becoming shallow now with his own arousal.

His hands reach the inside of her thighs starting at her knees. He moved upwards, and she began to arch in anticipation. In the past, she would not have enjoyed this seduction. Too much would be swirling in her head: shame brought on by endless indoctrination that sex is bad, worrying about this man's intentions. In the past, there was only muted joy in the act. Not this time—not with him.

She feels the moistness between her thighs increase as he inches closer. He suddenly grabs her by the arm and twists her toward the floor. She instinctively closes her eyes. Her fear is gone. He has made love to her before—with his words, with his poetry, and with his music. No one quite understands her like he does.

Christian lays her gently on the floor, her eyes still closed. She feels his hands move her nightgown toward her stomach. He kisses her thigh, and again, and again, and she can feel his hot breath on her pudenda—but he passes and moves to her stomach. Anna knows that he knows she wants him, but he lets the anticipation build. Right then Christian kisses her squarely on the mouth. It is a gentle kiss, a prolonged kiss.

She can feel Christian's manhood between her legs seeking its destination. She reaches down and grasps its enormity as she gently guides it into her. At first their movements are slow, back and forth, then quicker. Her breath becomes deeper and louder and faster. Her body aches as the pleasure and pain of his thrusting rushes toward each other and converges into a body-shattering orgasm.

Bang! She opens her eyes. Anna sits up in bed, disoriented and confused. She hears the sound of a trash bin lid slamming shut and realizes it was just her neighbor in the alley. As she comes to her senses, she realizes that Christian was just a dream. She sighs, feeling a sense of disappointment wash over her as she remembers their deep conversations and the strong connection they shared, even though they had never met in person. She lies back in bed, feeling a sense of disappointment and longing as she remembers the vivid details of the dream and the energy that had flowed between them.

She lays her head upon her pillow once more and desperately tries to recapture his presence. Anna falls asleep easily, the way sleep used to come to her as a child, innocent and dream-filled. There is no remorse, no doubt that being with Christian is good and right. She still feels his arms around her, her head cushioned against his chest as she drifts off, her body completely empty of tension.

When she wakes later and rises to face the day, to shower, to work—she thinks of him again and cannot bear the thought that this seduction was just a dream. She needs the physicality of his touch. Christian is animalistic in his innocence and ethereal in his purity. Anna can feel it surrounding her, and it makes her strong.

She must see Christian, she thinks. She must directly experience the passion that his sensuality has stirred in her. She smiles knowing she can make it happen—it must happen. Until then, she will reluctantly settle for Christian's words, his poetry, his music, and virtual visits in cyberspace—and in her dreams.